Take Time *Karl Williams*

Take time to think
It is the source of power.
Take time to read,
It is the foundation of wisdom

Take time to play,
It is the secret of staying young.
Take time to be quiet,
It is the opportunity to seek God.

Take time to be aware,
It is the opportunity to help others.
Take time to love and be loved,
It is God's greatest gift.

Take time to laugh,
It is the music of the soul.
Take time to be friendly,
It is the road to happiness.

Take time to dream,
It is what the future is made of.
Take time to pray,
It is the greatest power on earth.

There is time for everything.

G RATEFUL THANKS to the many generous people who were kind enough to share their profound knowledge and insight into the story of Knock with me. People like Monsignor Michael Walsh, Monsignor Dominick Grealy, Pat Lavelle and the staff of Knock Shrine, Sr Angela Forde, Dr Diarmuid Murray, Tom Neary, Jim O'Connell, and a most amazing woman – Mrs Judy Coyne.

Special thanks to my daily fellow pilgrims – Paul, Emily, Pauline, Nathan and James.

Eileen Good

Contents

Foreword

THE AUTHOR of this book set out to give the reader a bird's-eye view of Knock Shrine, how it began, how it has developed and how it is now. She has succeeded admirably in doing exactly that.

Of the one and a half million people who visit Knock Shrine every year, I feel that only a small percentage actually see all the buildings and all the grounds, and fewer still know all the services available to pilgrims and all that is happening.

It is mainly for that reason that I think Eileen Good has answered a need – to provide the reader with an easy-to-read, concise account of the principal events at Knock since 1879 and to give the reader a taste of the peace and tranquility that can be experienced by a sincere pilgrim to the Shrine.

I highly recommend this condensed story of Knock Shrine, which is so colourfully interspersed with photographs.

Monsignor Dominick Grealy, PP
Knock

We greet you, hand-maid of the Lord,

On whom the Power of God did rest;

Be with us, believers,

Gathered in prayer,

And implore for us

The gift of the spirit.

Antiphon to the Blessed Virgin Mary – Liturgy of the Hours (Terce)
St Mary's Abbey, Glencairn, Co. Waterford.

IT WAS A silent Apparition in Knock in 1879. That evening, the only sound was the lashing rain driven by a strong south-westerly gale sweeping across the village. Suddenly there was another sound – people running, splashing through the pools of water to gather near the gable wall of the church. At first a small group, then a total of fourteen villagers stood huddled together, staring, pointing at the wall. Half a mile away a farmer in his field stopped tending his animals and stared across at the church.

They had never seen anything like it. The gable wall of the church was a pool of light. The light was golden – bright, luminous, extraordinary. The people stood in the soaking rain, looking and then naming the figures enveloped in the beautiful light. The figures were life-size. The Blessed Virgin Mary stood with St Joseph on her right and St John the Evangelist on her left. On a plain altar there was a young lamb standing in front of a large cross. Angels hovered, wings fluttering, over the lamb. They had never imagined anything like it.

As they stared, details of the figures became more obvious and familiar. All of them recognised the Blessed Virgin and St Joseph. Giving their testimonies of that evening – August 21st 1879 – to the first formal commission set up in the weeks following the Apparition, they all agreed that the Blessed Virgin was wearing a long, white robe fastened at the neck. She had her hands raised to the level of her shoulders with the palms facing each other slanting inwards towards her face. Her eyes looked to heaven and she seemed to be praying. Thirteen-year-old Patrick Hill, who was watching with his friend John Durkan, described 'a brilliant crown on her head, and over the forehead where the crown fitted the brow, a beautiful rose'. He lifted up six-year-old John Curry to give him a better view.

The heavy rain and wind continued. The villagers were wet through and the ground around them was soaking. The rain stopped before reaching the figures and the ground around them was completely dry. One of the visionaries, Bríd Ní Thrinsigh (Bridget Trench) confirmed this when she ran forward to kiss the Blessed Virgin's feet – she testified later 'I felt the ground carefully with my hands and it was perfectly dry'. Bríd was seventy-five at the time of the Apparition and greeted the Blessed Virgin in her native Irish.

> *Sé do Bheatha Mhuire – Céad míle buidheachas le Dia agus leis an Maighdean Ghlórmhair a thug dúinn an taisbeánadh seo.*
> (A hundred thousand thanks to God and the glorious Virgin for this manifestation)

Mary McLoughlin was Archdeacon Cavanagh's housekeeper. That night she had gone to visit Mrs Byrne. She later recalled seeing figures and wondering if new statues had been delivered for the church. It was only when walking home, accompanied by Mrs Byrne's daughter Mary, that they both realised they were not looking at statues – they were figures! Mary Byrne dashed back to bring out her mother, her brother Dominick, her sister Margaret and her niece Catherine Murray. Dominick ran for his cousin Patrick, and his older cousin, Dominick Senior. She then hurried over to Judith Campbell's house and they both ran to the church. Mrs Flatley was passing along the road by the church and saw the figures quite clearly. Patrick Walsh, the farmer, still stood in his field and continued to stare over at the light.

As Mary Byrne gazed at the figure on the Blessed Virgin's left she was reminded of a statue she had seen in Lecanvey Church, near Westport. It was

'The Lamb, Altar and Cross of the Apparition
clearly signify the Paschal Mystery of Christ,
both the earthly liturgy of the Mass and heavenly
liturgy of which the Mass is a foretaste.'
Monsignor Michael Walsh –
The Glory of Knock

the figure of St John. She noted that he was now wearing a mitre that she did not recognise. Many years later when she was giving details of the figures to Mrs Coyne – who was researching details for the carving of the Shrine statues – she recalled that St John appeared to be preaching, not reading, and he appeared to be preaching about the Lamb. The Lamb was the focal point of this silent Apparition.

The other witnesses assisted Judith Campbell when she ran to her mother who had collapsed outside her house. When they returned to the wall, there was nothing to be seen. The night rain was lashing against the dark, vacant wall.

Next morning, word of the Apparition spread rapidly. The parish priest of Knock at that time was Archdeacon Cavanagh. He was well known as a devout man, and a tireless campaigner on behalf of the poor. His housekeeper had gone back to the house on the night of the Apparition, but he paid little attention to her story and did not go down to the church. This was a decision he always regretted. In an interview with the *Weekly News* on 14 February 1880, he recorded

> I console myself with the reflection that it was the will
> of God that the Apparition should be shown to the people,
> not to the priest.

He had great devotion to the souls in purgatory.

> It would seem as if this devotion, and devotion to the Holy Mother of God were inseparable.

Several months before the Apparition, Archdeacon Cavanagh completed his great wish to offer one hundred Masses for the souls in purgatory. It was after the last of these Masses was offered that the Apparition took place at Knock on 21 August 1879.

Following the Apparition, the fourteen witnesses were questioned by two official Church Commissions of Enquiry. The first was just weeks after the Apparition in 1879. The second was with the surviving witnesses in 1936. In each case the Church Authorities were satisfied that the accounts reported were authentic and noted that

> the testimony of the witnesses, taken as a whole, was trustworthy and satisfactory.

Following the second enquiry, Father James Fergus, Secretary of the Commission, entrusted the documents to Frank Duff, founder of the Legion of Mary, who brought them to Rome.

Today it would be dubbed a multi-media event. In 1879 it personified tranquility and hope in a dejected, desolate corner of Ireland.

It was a silent Apparition. That very silence continues to be the call to go there and ponder the mystery within. For those who cannot hear, the silence of the sacred penetrates and communicates the loudest message. For those who cannot see, the very sacredness of the place invites meditation and reflection on the deep and profound silence that was the core of an extraordinary event in the lives of very ordinary people.

Our Lady, St Joseph, St John the Evangelist, the Lamb, the Cross and the Angels – communicate powerful reflections on 'the glory of heaven'
  Monsignor Michael Walsh – *The Glory of Knock*

Knock, like every authentic Marian Shrine, draws us to Christ and through Him to the life of the Trinity. And the Irish tradition has long seen Mary as *Bean Tí na Trionoide*
  Christopher O'Donnell OCarm – *The Meaning of Knock*

Prayer to Our Lady of Knock

Our Lady of Knock, Queen of Ireland, you gave hope to your people in a time of distress and comforted them in sorrow. You have inspired countless pilgrims to pray with confidence to your Son, remembering His promise; 'Ask and you shall receive, seek and you shall find.'

Help me to remember that we are all pilgrims on the road to heaven. Fill me with love and concern for my brothers and sisters in Christ, especially those who live with me.

Comfort me when I am sick or lonely or depressed. Teach me how to take part ever more reverently in the holy Mass. Pray for me now, and at the hour of my death. Amen.

Our Lady of Knock, pray for us.

God is the light behind the distant hill, a light which

beckons us forward into a future which

will hold many surprises, joyful and sorrowful, but

which leads to the final glory of the

absolute future which is the vision and peace

of God himself.

Fr Gabriel Daly

Pilgrimage

I N TODAY's world of instant technology, constant news and analysis, the notion of making a journey to a place apart, to experience the unknown, can provoke raised eyebrows.

Yet it is that very desire to take time out, to find solitude, that speaks to our deepest need to find a place apart. To know solitude, yet to experience the communicating bond of shared silence in a sacred place is to know we have arrived. We can be renewed in spirit in a place where for years the worn and weary have gathered to be refreshed. For thousands of years the area around Knock was revered as a holy place. In the Summer of 1838 the Ordnance Survey documented the finding of *Tobar Caolainne* – Keelan's Well in the townland of Caldragh – and noted

> that the stations were performed at the well on Garland Sunday – a nice marriage of an early Christian cult stretching back well over a thousand years with a pre-Christian festival (Lughnasa) which may well be at least a thousand years older still.
> Nollaig Ó Muraile – *Survival or Salvation – A Second Mayo Book of Theology*

Pilgrims came to Knock within hours of the Apparition. The curious, the sick, the infirm, all travelled to see the spot and touch the gable wall of the church. The village church had to be kept open continuously, but still could not contain the unceasing stream of pilgrims. Within a short time, word had spread throughout Connaught and then to the entire country. Newspaper reports of the day, both in Ireland and England, reported on the extraordinary happenings at Knock and added to people's desire to see the place where Our Lady had chosen to appear.

Knock circa 1920

In March 1880, fifty-two members of the Holy Name Confraternity from the Redemptorist Church in Limerick were the first organised pilgrimage to travel to Knock Shrine. They travelled by train to Tuam and then on to Knock using nine open sidecars. They presented Archdeacon Cavanagh with a banner which was placed in the sanctuary of the church. In August of the same year a further pilgrimage of five hundred members from the same Confraternity travelled to Knock.

In 1880 Archdeacon Cavanagh erected the altar in the church, presented by the pilgrims from Cork city. It is a replica of the white marble altar in the Carmelite Church in Clarendon Street, Dublin. Numbers continued to grow as pilgrims came from all around the country. In August 1882 a pilgrimage

Knock circa 1920

of nine hundred pilgrims came from Manchester in England – the overseas outreach had begun. Archbishop Murphy travelled from Tasmania, Archbishop Clune from Perth, Australia and Archbishop Lynch from Toronto, Canada. His account of his visit includes his reaction to the conditions of the people living in the area at the time. Evicted families, deserted houses and bad land led him to comment that

> It was a most merciful condescension on the part of our Immaculate Mother to appear in the neighbourhood of such a place, and to give the patience and courage of saints and martyrs to these poor people.
> *Knock Shrine*

As the numbers increased, life in the little village of Knock and in the surrounding countryside was changing completely. Hotels and lodging-houses in towns on the railway line – Ballyhaunis and Claremorris – were constantly full. Within a year of the Apparition, the gable wall of the church was completely stripped of cement: it had been taken by pilgrims. Instead, the wall was covered by crutches left by them in thanksgiving for cures received.

The inscription on the stone in the west wall of the old parish church completed in 1828 reads

> My house shall be called a house of prayer to all nations (Matt. 11)
> This is the gate of the Lord
> the just shall enter into it. (Ps. 117 (118))

The church is dedicated to St John the Baptist who proclaimed

> Behold the Lamb of God

In view of the subsequent events and the development of Knock as a world shrine, many people regard these words as prophetic.

In the immediate years following the Apparition, Knock continued to grow in stature as a Marian Shrine. Then, for a period, numbers started to decline until the fiftieth anniversary of the Apparition, August 1929, which marked a new era for the Shrine. For the first time an organised pilgrimage was welcomed and addressed by an archbishop of the archdiocese of Tuam. The pilgrims were from the St Michan's Conference of St Vincent de Paul in

Handmaids and stewards, circa 1940

Dublin and were welcomed by Dr Thomas Gilmartin of Tuam. His participation was a historic moment in the history of the Shrine.

In 1935, on the fifty-sixth Anniversary of the Apparition, a most significant event took place in the old schoolhouse. On that evening the Knock Shrine Society of Handmaids, Stewards and Promoters was founded by Liam Coyne and his wife Judy Coyne and approved by the Archbishop, Dr Gilmartin. To this day the service and commitment of these volunteers remains at the very core of the success of every pilgrimage to Knock.

That evening the procession of thousands of pilgrims holding lighted candles prompted the *Connaught Tribune* headline on 31 August 1935

> INSPIRING MAYO SCENES
> LIGHTED CANDLE PROCESSION
> SOCIETY FOR RECOGNITION FORMED.

One of the happiest people present on that night must have been visionary Mary O'Connell (Mary Byrne) then eighty-five years old and still able to take part in the devotions. Despite her age and illness she was always willing to meet pilgrims and retell her story. Her grandson, Jim O'Connell, has clear recollections of his grandmother. He remembers her going to daily Mass, and always visiting the Apparition Wall at the church. Every Christmas Eve she would take him and his brothers and sisters to the church to visit the crib and then to the local shop to select a small toy as their Christmas present. Mary was a Child of Mary and when she died on 19 October 1936 she was laid out in her blue cloak.

The Diamond Jubilee in 1939 saw the greatest pilgrimage to date at the Shrine. In total, one hundred and seventy thousand pilgrims visited the shrine during that year – the year in which Archbishop Gilmartin died on 14 October.

On 18 August 1946 Fr Patrick J. Peyton CSC, the Rosary Priest, a native of County Mayo and well known on American radio at the time, held a Rosary Rally at the Shrine. The Knock Shrine Rosary Crusade was formally launched on 18 May 1947 and the pilgrims were addressed by Fr James Horan CC Aghamore, who later became quite famous as Monsignor Horan, Parish Priest of Knock.

One million pilgrims travelled to Knock in 1954 – The Marian Year. Twenty-five thousand children – including many invalids – came on the National Childrens' Pilgrimage on 9 May of that year. The largest single pilgrimage in the Shrine's seventy-five year history was when fifty thousand members of the Pioneer Total Abstinence Association gathered at the Shrine on Sunday, 19 September 1954. They travelled by twenty-two trains, four hundred and four buses, seven thousand cars, by bicycle, or on foot.

The first National Public Novena in honour of Our Lady of Knock, was held from 14 to 22 August 1977. This annual pilgrimage is still one of the greatest occasions in the Knock Shrine calendar.

Monsignor Dominick Grealy – Parish Priest at Knock Shrine – is constantly aware of the great Faith of the pilgrims at Knock. He uses the word 'reverence' to describe the atmosphere at the Shrine on any given day –

Ireland v Wales

Venue: Aviva Stadium **Kick-off:** Today, 2.15pm **On TV:** Live on TV3, UTV

(Leinster) **Rob Kearney**	15	**Leigh Halfpenny** (Scarlets)
(Munster) **Keith Earls**	14	**Liam Williams** (Saracens)
(Munster) **Chris Farrell**	13	**Scott Williams** (Scarlets)
(Connacht) **Bundee Aki**	12	**Hadleigh Parkes** (Scarlets)
(Ulster) **Jacob Stockdale**	11	**Steff Evans** (Scarlets)
(Leinster) **Johnny Sexton**	10	**Dan Biggar** (Ospreys)
(Munster) **Conor Murray**	9	**Gareth Davies** (Scarlets)
(Leinster) **Cian Healy**	1	**Rob Evansa** (Scarlets)
(Ulster, c) **Rory Best**	2	**Ken Owens** (Scarlets)
(Leinster) **Andrew Porter**	3	**Samson Lee** (Scarlets)
(Leinster) **Devin Toner**	4	**Cory Hill** (Dragons)
(Leinster) **James Ryan**	5	**Alun-Wyn Jones** (Ospreys, c)
(Munster) **Peter O'Mahony**	6	**Aaron Shingler** (Scarlets)
(Leinster) **Dan Leavy**	7	**Josh Navidi** (Cardiff)
(Munster) **C J Stander**	8	**Ross Moriarty** (Gloucester)

Replacements: S Cronin (Leinster), J McGrath (Leinster), John Ryan (Munster), Q Roux (Connacht), J Conan (Leinster), K Marmion (Connacht), J Carbery (Leinster), F McFadden (Leinster)

Replacements: E Dee (Dragons), W Jones (Scarlets), T Francis (Exeter), B Davies (Ospreys), J Tipuric (Ospreys), A Davies (Scarlets), G Anscombe (Cardiff), G North (Northampton).

Referee: Glen Jackson (NZ).
Assistant referees: Pascal Gauzere (Fra), Matthew Carley (Eng).
TMO: Rowan Kitt (Eng)

	USB Host:	
	USB Device:	Unblock
	Option I/F:	Unblock
		Unblock

Memory

Standard Size:	256.0 MB
Option Slot:	0 Bytes
Total Size:	256.0 MB

Emulation

Emulation:	PCL6
Default Font:	Courier
Default Code Set:	IBM PC-8

Scan Settings

File Format:	PDF
Resolution:	300x300dpi
Quality:	Text+Photo

Counters

Copier	43810
Printer	4568
Total	**48378**
Paper Size	
A4	48376
B5	0
A5	0
Folio	2
Legal	0
Letter	0
Statement	0
Other1	0
Other2	0
Scanned Pages	
Copier	18191
Other	0
Total	**18191**

Toner Gauge
WARNING

We recommend the use of our own brand supplies.
We will not be liable for any damage caused by the
use of third party supplies in this machine.

bled

ed
200 Mode

nutes
conds
ed

led
stalled
stalled

nected

c

d
ned
ned
ned

ed
ed
ed
ed

'This solitude does not separate me from others: it helps me love them more tenderly, realistically and attentively. I begin to distinguish between the false solitude which is a flight from others to be alone with egoism, sadness and a bruised sensitivity, and true solitude which is a communion with God and with others'

Jean Vanier – *Community and Growth*

whether it is the pilgrim alone seeking solitude or the organised group bound together by shared problems, hopes, stories and prayers. The great strength of Knock is, he says, that in today's hectic world it offers an opportunity to experience peace and quiet in the healing atmosphere of support and encouragement.

Ever since pilgrims have come to Knock they have done the Stations of the Cross and recited the Rosary while walking around the outside of the old church. This became known as the traditional station of Knock. It is a combination of the ancient Irish pilgrimage of 'doing the rounds' at holy places, which dates from the time of St Patrick, and traditional devotion to Our Lady while reflecting on the mysteries of the Rosary. Pilgrims have always wanted to experience the very spot where Our Lady appeared by touching the stone at the gable wall. Today, people can still do this by touching a section of the original Apparition Gable which has been encased in the front wall of the new Shrine Enclosure.

The most important section of any organised pilgrimage is the invalids who travel to the Shrine. The Sodality of the 'Volunteers of Suffering' was established at Knock Shrine in 1961 by the Archbishop of Tuam for all invalids who are prepared to offer their sufferings to God in order to help others. These volunteers can assist at public devotions held especially for them at the Shrine on the last Thursday of each month from May to September.

'Behold the Lamb of God' was how St John the Baptist introduced Jesus at the start of his public life. The significance of the Lamb at the Apparition,

The Stations of the Cross

and the Eucharistic connection, invites pilgrims to consider the Mass and Holy Communion as the culmination of their Knock Pilgrimage.

Pilgrims travel daily to Knock. Organised pilgrimages are increasing each season from both national and international centres. By its very location, deep in the west of Ireland, the journey to Knock from anywhere is a pilgrimage. For most people, Knock is not a place one happens to be passing through – arriving there is the result of a decision to take time to journey, to go apart to experience the sacred and hopefully make the return journey renewed in spirit. For those who interrupt their journey to visit the Shrine, very often the 'stop' becomes a regular habit.

> Pilgrimage to a shrine like Knock must never become a way of escaping the problems of the world, but in the great tradition of Irish pilgrimage it should awaken in pilgrims a renewed sense of communion with those strangers who are hungry, oppressed, downtrodden and rejected ... and of course, the pilgrim grows in awareness that on life's journey there are no strangers, only fellow pilgrims.
>
> Michael Drumm – *The Meaning of Knock*

Remember, O most loving Virgin Mary,

That never was it known

That anyone who fled to your protection

Implored your help, or sought your intercession,

Was left unaided.

Inspired by this confidence

I fly unto you, Virgin of virgins, my Mother

To you do I come, before you I stand,

sinful and sorrowful

O Mother of the Word Incarnate,

despise not my petitions

But in your clemency

Graciously hear and answer me. Amen.

F ROM AS EARLY as April 1880 letters from grateful pilgrims poured into Knock Shrine. The first recorded cure in Archdeacon Cavanagh's diary is the cure, on 31 August 1879, of twelve-year-old Delia Gordan from Claremorris from deafness. Other letters came from America, Tasmania, England, Scotland and all over Ireland, giving detailed accounts of cures. Sight and hearing restored, lameness cured, heart trouble resolved, depression lifted – and many more. So many were the letters received by Archdeacon Cavanagh, Parish Priest of Knock at that time, that he found it necessary to write to the Editor of *The Freeman's Journal* in February 1880:

> Sir – I will be obliged if you will make known to my numerous correspondents that it is simply impossible for me to answer the vast number of letters that arrive here daily from every part of Ireland, England and Scotland, relative to the Apparition of our Blessed Immaculate Mother.
>
> I take this opportunity of stating that the report given in the public journals are substantially correct, both as regards the Apparition and the numerous miracles wrought here since the 21st of last August,
> I remain,
> Yours faithfully
> Bartholomew Cavanagh PP

Many of today's pilgrims can recall visiting Knock as young children, with their parents and possibly grandparents, not realising that each visit was probably for a 'special intention'. Since the first local pilgrims travelled to the Shrine back in 1879, to today's international pilgrims, petitions still hinge around prayers for healing of mind and body, for peace and harmony within the family, and possibly most of all in today's world, for the grace and faith to be able to 'make sense of it all'.

Every day at Knock Shrine you will see people visiting the Knock Shrine Office to get Mass Cards signed. In many cases these will be for the departed soul of a loved one, for others it will be to include in the most special way possible one of the many problems that most families today have to grapple with.

Dear God, why me?
Why do I have cancer?/Why is my child doing drugs?
Why did my parents split up?/What will I do with my life?/
Why was I made redundant?/Why does alcohol rule my life?/
Why am I so unhappy?/
Why did God let my beloved child take his own life?/
Who can I tell I'm pregnant?/Why does he or she not love me any more?/
Are you really there Lord?/I'm so lonely –
that's why I'm here.

Many people who come on pilgrimage will be concerned that they don't know how to pray – what to say. The reality of Knock is that this doesn't matter.

Coming to Knock and stepping into the shrine grounds is leaving the ordinary circumstances of life, and stepping into a place where faith is foremost. It is the crossing of a threshold, the entrance to a space where countless thousands have prayed for more than a hundred years. This is holy ground. There are Masses, Rosaries, processions, hymns and prayers. Everything else falls into the background, and God and His power to heal, through the intercession of Our Lady of Knock, comes into sharp focus.

Sr Angela Forde – *The Meaning of Knock*

Knock is probably the only Marian Shrine in the world where there is a Prayer Guidance Centre, in which pilgrims can experience new ways of deepening their prayer life. In the centre are three beautiful prayer rooms in which several sessions of guided prayer, based on scripture, are conducted daily during the pilgrimage season. These sessions are conducted by leaders who have been trained by the Jesuit team in Manresa House in Dublin. Many pilgrims, lay as well as religious, now avail of the facilities in the Prayer Guidance Centre and the eighty acres of landscaped Shrine grounds to make a few days prayerful retreat and to escape from the worries of everyday life. Special sessions are also conducted for young people and for children by the full-time Youth Director.

On the day of a large pilgrimage, to be present in the Basilica during the Sacrament of the Sick is to witness a moment of grace. It is not just those who are unable to walk to the priest who receive the Sacrament, all those present who are in need can partake of it. As the priest says:

> Through this holy anointing
> may the Lord in his love and mercy help you
> with the grace of the Holy Spirit. Amen.
> May the Lord who frees you from sin
> save you and raise you up. Amen.

The sick describe that moment as receiving a sense of great peace and contentment, while those present with them are aware of contributing hope, love and prayers. By their solidarity and compassion with the sick, the congregation can share in their pain and suffering and hopefully be a source

'Through this holy anointing
may the Lord in his love and mercy help you
with the grace of the Holy Spirit. Amen.
May the Lord who frees you from sin
save you and raise you up. Amen.'

of courage and reconciliation. Physical cures may or may not be the outcome of their visit, inner strength and renewed hope, in communion with others present, is often the healing that provides nourishment for the return journey.

One of the great traditions in Knock is the practice of going to confession. Despite an overall trend of declining numbers partaking of this sacrament, being present in Knock would seem to be an influential factor in people's decision to seek God's forgiveness. During the pilgrimage season as many as six thousand people go to confession each week, a service made possible by a rota of over two hundred priests willing to be available to the Shrine for confessions. At the all night vigil of 7/8 December 2001, forty-four priests heard confessions from 10pm to midnight.

It was these very numbers that made it necessary to provide a Chapel of Reconciliation, dedicated to the sole purpose of providing a setting of peace and forgiveness for these pilgrims. Following a major architectural competition for the design of the chapel, organised with the support of the Royal Institute of Architects of Ireland, the winning design was awarded to Architects de Blacam & Meagher.

In July 1990, on the occasion of the dedication of the Chapel of Reconciliation, Dr Joseph Cassidy accurately described the building, relating it to the approaching pilgrim:

> It bows its head a bit, hunches its shoulders. It goes down in its knees, snuggles into the earth, prostrates itself before God in humility and self-effacement.

'May this building be a source of healing of the countless wounds that afflict us all – physical, mental and spiritual. May it be a haven of peace, a rest for souls, a Chapel of Reconciliation with God and neighbour.'

Monsignor Grealey

Having Confessed *Patrick Kavanagh*

Having confessed he feels
That he should go down on his knees and pray
For forgiveness for his pride, for having
Dared to view his soul from the outside.
Lie at the heart of the emotion, time
Has its own work to do. We must not anticipate
Or awaken for a moment. God cannot catch us
Unless we stay in the unconscious room
Of our hearts. We must be nothing,
Nothing that God may make us something.
We must not touch the immortal material
We must not daydream to-morrow's judgement-
God must be allowed to surprise us.
We have sinned, sinned like Lucifer
By this anticipation. Let us lie down again
Deep in anonymous humility and God
May find us worthy material for His hand.

Approaching the chapel is the line of Holy Water Fonts, designed by well-known sculptor Imogen Stuart, linking the way to reconciliation with a reminder of the baptismal use of water in cleansing sin. Water is the theme common to all the fonts, which depict scenes from the lives of the saints and biblical scenes.

A further benefit of the Chapel of Reconciliation is the provision of a professional counselling service within the building. Staffed by a professional counselling psychologist, assisted by a team of trained counsellors, the service is available to everyone on a 'drop in' basis. Originally a part-time service, the demands were such that it was necessary to provide the full time service that now exists.

The emotional wear and tear of today's modern world, where time and support from family and friends is not always available, can block out hope and leave instead an aching pain of confusion and inadequacy. The availability of trained personnel, their commitment to give that most precious commodity – time – in an atmosphere of care and confidentiality is a natural extension of the healing graces synonymous with Knock.

> Here is the place
> You would want to arrive at
> After a long journey preceded
> By grief and much delay.
> Angela Greene – *Silence and the Blue Night*

O Lord my God, I cried to you

For help,

And you have healed me.

You have turned my mourning

Into dancing;

You have taken off my sackcloth and clothed

Me with joy,

So that my soul may praise you and not be

Silent.

O Lord my God, I will give thanks to you

Forever.

Psalm 30:2, 11-12

THE INCREASE in numbers visiting Knock, from the humble beginnings of the first organised pilgrimage – when fifty-two pilgrims travelled to Knock Shrine – to today's numbers of over one and a half million pilgrims each year, would be for many the definition of a miracle.

Over the years, the Shrine calendar has been marked by displays of great public devotion, inspiring moments of belief and prayers, linking pilgrims from around the world.

There have been many recorded highlights of significant times for the Shrine down through the years. The Marian Year of 1954 was one such occasion. On November 1st of that year – All Saints Day – the Archbishop of Tuam, Dr Joseph Walsh, represented the Shrine in St Peter's Basilica in Rome when Pope Pius XII proclaimed the new feast of Our Lady Queen and solemnly crowned the statue of Our Lady and Child – *Salus Populi Romani* ('Salvation of the Roman People').

Ten years later – 21 November 1964 – twenty-four bishops celebrated Mass with Pope Paul VI to conclude the 3rd session of the Second Vatican Council. All the bishops present were invited from the most famous Marian Shrines in the world. By including Most Rev. Dr Joseph Walsh, Archbishop of Tuam, as the representative of Knock Shrine, the Pope acknowledged to the world the significance of Knock as a Marian Shrine.

The planning for the Centenary of the Apparition was launched at the opening of the pilgrimage season in 1970. The overall planning and responsibility for the commemorative year rested in the capable hands of the then parish priest of Knock – James Horan. A man of fierce determination, of unshakable faith and belief in Knock, he directed himself and those around him with boundless enthusiasm. He never faltered in his belief that everything was possible. Those involved with him in the countless projects that needed attention speak of a man of extraordinary energy and ideas, who was above all passionate in his devotion and dedication to Knock. The initial and most extensive project was the decision to build a new church to accommodate the thousands of pilgrims now travelling to the Shrine. The church was also to provide first-class facilities for the increasing number of invalids participating in the pilgrimages. It was envisaged that the church would accommodate ten thousand people. When asked about the feasibility of such a project being finished on time, with a twinkle in his eye, he would reply, 'Well it'll have to be ready! Won't the Pope be coming?' And so the process began – for the building and 'The Visit'.

Architects Louis Brennan, Brian Brennan and Daithí Hanly were commissioned to design and build the new church. The first sod was turned on 6 November 1973. The foundation stone, blessed by Pope Paul VI, was laid by Dr Cunnane on 15 August 1974. On 18 July 1976 the completed building was dedicated to Our Lady Queen of Ireland by Archbishop Cunnane, assisted by Archbishop Ryan of Dublin and Archbishop Morris of Cashel and Emly, in the presence of Cardinal Conway and the Bishops of Ireland.

The church covers an area of just over one acre, and is the site of the Byrne cottage, where five of the visionaries lived. It is basically circular in shape, divided into five chapels. Each chapel is designed to ensure that all pilgrims have an unobstructed view of the high altar, with the area immediately around the sanctuary reserved for invalids.

Basilica designed by architects Louis Brennan, Brian Brennan and Daithí Hanley

There was, however, an unexpected and unofficial opening of the new church on Sunday 16 May 1976. It was the day of the pilgrimage from the Diocese of Achonry led by Bishop James Fergus, with the choir from the Church of the Holy Family, Kiltimagh. Bishop Fergus had been Secretary to the second commission of Enquiry of the Visionaries in 1936. With them were Capuchin Pilgrimages from Dublin, Cork and Donegal.

It was an appalling day – not dissimilar to the Apparition Day. It rained continuously. The pilgrims were soaking wet. Because of the weather conditions, Monsignor Horan took the decision to open the doors of the new church and let the people in. The church was not ready to receive pilgrims and there was no seating, but a big table was brought in and used as an altar. As the church filled up, the first congregation burst into spontaneous song, filling the new church with the first hymn of praise to Mary.

On the Feast of the Annunciation, 25 March 1979 the new church was solemnly consecrated – marking the opening of the Centenary celebrations.

That year was truly a year of celebration. The number of pilgrimages was the highest ever recorded. Schools, parishes, dioceses, national organisations, special devotional groups, all came to mark the hundreth anniversary. The contrast in times could hardly have been greater; the crowds of people travelling in comfort from all over the world and the facilities available to them. But what had not changed was their belief and devotion, and perhaps most of all their delight in celebrating a unique event that had stood the test of time.

In April, Pope John Paul II sent a special videotaped message to the National Missionary Congress held at Knock. It was a unique gathering of missionaries from all parts of the world.

The annual novena, 14 to 22 August, attracted immense crowds. On 15 August – the Feast of the Assumption – Church and State dignitaries from all over the world attended Mass in the new church to celebrate the centenary of the Apparition. RTÉ televised the Mass live throughout Europe. August 21, the actual anniversary date of the Apparition, was a most inspiring day of thanksgiving and prayer for the honour and blessings bestowed on the village of Knock one hundred years previously.

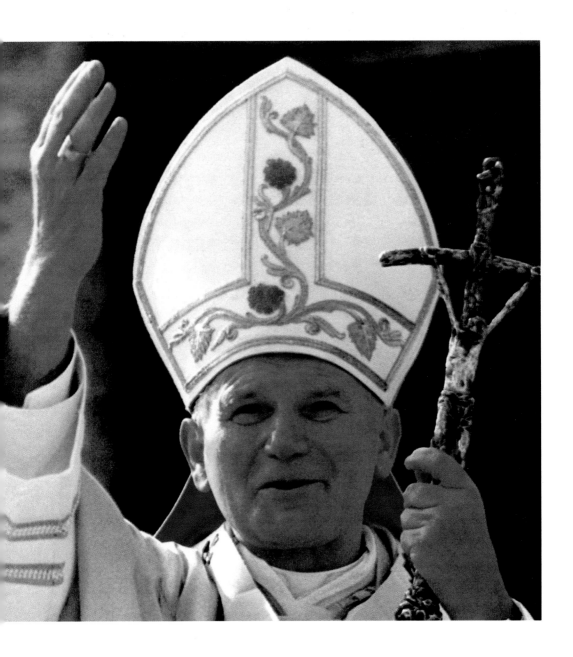

Here I am at the goal of my journey to Ireland: the Shrine of our Lady at Knock. Since I first learned of the centenary of this Shrine, which is being celebrated this year, I have felt a strong desire to come here, the desire to make yet another pilgrimage to the Shrine of the Mother of Christ, the Mother of the Church, the Queen of Peace.

I am here then as a pilgrim, a sign of the pilgrim Church throughout the world participating, through my presence as Peter's successor, in a very special way in the centenary celebration of this Shrine.

Pope John Paul II – Knock Shrine, 30 September 1979

With these words, Pope John Paul II greeted almost half a million people at Knock Shrine on 30 September 1979. It was the climax of the Centenary Celebrations. For many months, complex preparations had been afoot, with an extraordinary variety of agencies, clergy and volunteers to ensure the smooth running of this most memorable visit. Over half a million people travelled to the Shrine that day. Locals remember every road and field being packed with cars and buses and every possible vantage spot a sea of people. The appalling weather that day did nothing to dampen the uplifting, enthusiastic atmosphere that prevailed throughout the visit.

'*Céad míle fáilte romhat,* your Holiness!' was how Monsignor Horan greeted the Holy Father at Knock Shrine.

In the Church, the Pope laid his hands on the Sick, blessed them and in his homily told them

> to love the sick is something that the Church has learned from Christ. Today I am happy to be with the sick and the handicapped. I have come to give witness to Christ's love for you, and to tell you that the Church and the Pope love you too ... Your call to suffering requires strong faith and patience. Yes, it means that you are called to love with a special intensity. But remember that Our Blessed Mother, Mary, is close to you, just as she was close to Jesus at the foot of the cross. And she will never leave you alone.

He had a special message for the Handmaids and Stewards of Knock Shrine and the Directors of pilgrimages

> I know from firsthand experience the value of the services you render to make every pilgrim feel at home at this Shrine, and to help them to make every visit a loving and prayerful encounter with Mary, the Mother of Divine Grace. In a special way, you are the servants of the Mother of Jesus ... You are also servants of your brothers and sisters. In helping and guiding the many pilgrims and especially the sick and handicapped, you perform not only a work of charity but also a task of evangelisation ... I pray for you, I thank you, and I invoke upon you abundant graces of goodness and holiness of life. Receive the blessing which I cordially extend to you and all your loved ones.

The Pope then honoured the Handmaids and Stewards by requesting that a Spiritual Bouquet, presented to him by them, should always be kept at the Shrine as a tribute to their faith and loyalty to the Holy See.

Acknowledging the significance of the year, Pope John Paul ɪɪ told the thousands present

> All those who have come here have received blessings through the intercession of Mary. From that Day of Grace, the twenty-first of August 1879, until this very day, the sick and suffering, people handicapped in body or mind, troubled in their faith or their conscience, all have been healed, comforted and confirmed in their faith because they trusted that the Mother of God would lead them to her Son, Jesus. Every time a pilgrim comes up to what was once an obscure bogside village in County Mayo, every time a man, woman or child comes up to the old church with the Apparition Gable or to the new Shrine of Mary Queen of Ireland, it is to renew his or her faith in salvation that comes through Jesus, who made us all children of God and heirs to the Kingdom of Heaven. By entrusting yourselves to Mary, you receive Christ.

At the end of his Homily, the Pope consecrated Ireland and her people to Mary Mother of the Church for it was in her role as Mother of the Church that she appeared at Knock in 1879. He remembered the problems in Northern Ireland and prayed

> In a special way we entrust to you this great wound now afflicting our people, hoping that your hands will be able to cure and heal it.

The Pope then bestowed two great honours on the Shrine. He raised the new church to the status of Basilica – a title that only the Pope can confer. And immediately afterwards presented a Golden Rose to the Shrine. The Golden Rose is the most prestigious gift a Pope can bestow and is a gift of exceptional honour. Archbishop Cunnane received the gift on behalf of the Shrine. Then, like the thousands of pilgrims before him and since, the pilgrim Pope walked to the Shrine at the Apparition Gable where he knelt, prayed and lit a candle – a perpetual memorial of his visit and to emphasise the importance of Family Prayer.

The Papal visit was the outstanding success of the Centenary year. By the honours he conferred, his understanding and appreciation of the significance of the Apparition, the Pope made it abundantly clear that, on behalf of the Church, he was fully endorsing Knock Shrine as one of the major Marian Shrines in the world.

The cross, which was part of the outdoor altar erected for the Pope's Mass, now stands in the Shrine grounds as permanent memorial to the Centenary visit.

1981 saw the arrival in Knock of a most appropriate congregation of nuns – the Carmelites. 'Tranquilla', their convent, was opened on 15 October of that year. Their life of prayer, silence and devotion to the Eucharist seem to capture the very essence of the message of the Apparition and make their relocation to Knock most appropriate.

The Chapel of the Blessed Sacrament was designed by architects Taylor & Carr, and opened on the Feast of Corpus Christi, 1983. During the pilgrimage season (May to October) there is daily exposition of the Blessed Sacrament from after 11 am to 5 pm each day. This daily opportunity to pray in silent adoration in the presence of the Blessed Sacrament is one of the most fitting ways of reading and answering the message of the Apparition. The pilgrim can follow Our Lady's example of meditation

> Our Lady of Knock appears as contemplating and adoring the Eucharistic mystery. By her upraised eyes she is inviting us to do what she is doing. She would have us find in the Eucharistic celebration as a whole the totality and summit of Christian life which is the beginning of life eternal.
>
> *Knock Shrine Annual* 1959

The 1828 inscription on the west wall of the old parish church reads:

My house shall be called the House of Prayer to all nations

And that is exactly what happens today. All nations come to Knock to pray. It is the manner in which all nations travel to Knock that would cause those who chose that inscription to wonder at it. Pilgrims from all over the world now regularly fly into nearby Knock Airport and within minutes are kneeling at the gable wall, where the visionaries knelt over a hundred years ago. The extraordinary achievement of having an airport at Knock was the brainchild of Monsignor Horan. While realising its value in promoting Knock as an International Pilgrimage centre, he also recognised its value in improving the social, economic and industrial life of the people of the West of Ireland.

The Blessed Sacrament Chapel

Knock Airport.
(Photo © Tom Campbell)

The inaugural flights from the new airport – Horan International – to Rome, took place on 25 October 1985. The historic moment was witnessed by almost forty thousand people. The official opening took place on 30 May 1986. Two months later, Monsignor Horan, together with family and friends flew to Lourdes. While on pilgrimage there, he died suddenly. Monsignor Dominick Grealy remembers the day quite clearly. He was, at that time, Administor in Tuam, and on the morning of 1 August he was doing his First Friday rounds. He got a phone call from a shocked Archbishop Cunnane, 'James is gone!' he was told, 'You had better go down to Knock straight away to prepare for his funeral.' Monsignor Horan and Monsignor Grealy had been great friends. They golfed together, holidayed together – usually a last minute, surprise destination of Monsignor Horan's choosing – and they prayed together, always the Rosary at the end of the day.

His funeral was the first into Knock Airport. Thousands of people attended his funeral Mass in the Basilica, with Archbishop Cunnane as chief Celebrant. He is buried in the grounds of his beloved Basilica.

In such sad circumstances, Monsignor Dominick Grealy succeeded Monsignor Horan as Parish Priest of Knock and Director of the Shrine on 1 August 1986.

In 1990 and 1992 two further significant buildings were opened within the Shrine complex. The new Chapel of Reconciliation, spearheaded by Monsignor Grealy, was dedicated on 15 July 1990. The chief celebrant at the opening was Dr Joseph Cassidy, Archbishop of Tuam and His Excellency Archbishop Emmanuele Gerada, Apostolic Nuncio to Ireland presided. In spite of the growing trend of decreasing numbers going to confession, in

Knock the opposite is true. Every year the number of people wishing to go to confession has increased. Every day of the year, for five hours priests are available for confession and during the pilgrimage season the hours are extended – nine hours on Saturdays and eight on Sundays. Monsignor Grealy is lavish in his praise of the resident team of confessors in Knock, and the huge number of priests who come from their parishes on an organised basis to help. Added to this daily facility, is the opportunity for any person to meet with trained counsellors should they wish to avail of their help

In 1992 Monsignor Grealy realised that the oratory structure at the Apparition Gable Wall had become unsafe and that a new building would have to be erected. After much consultation and thought as to the most appropriate design for this important building, the project was undertaken by internationally-known architect, Andrzej Wejchert. Work commenced at the end of 1991 and the resulting Apparition Chapel was blessed and opened on 10 May 1992.

The constant stream of pilgrims to the Apparition Chapel every day is ongoing affirmation by them that it is a prayerful place. The Apparition figures were designed to a most detailed description, given by Mrs Coyne, founder of the Handmaids, to the renowned sculptor, Professor Ferri, in Rome. Mrs Coyne had spoken with one of the last visionaries, Mrs Mary O'Connell (Mary Byrne) who described each figure to her emphasizing their position, expression and clothing. By reflecting on the magnificent white Carrara marble figures, the pilgrim is instantly transposed to the evening of 21 August 1879.

On a most beautiful day, 5 June 1993, Mother Teresa of Calcutta came on a pilgrimage to Knock Shrine. She got an overwhelming reception from over fifty thousand pilgrims who welcomed her. A tiny, frail woman, she was welcomed and introduced to the invalids and pilgrims by Monsignor Grealy. During her visit she attended Mass at the outdoor altar of the Basilica, concelebrated by Archbishop Joseph Cassidy. She visited the Apparition Chapel and recited her 'Rosary for Life'. In his homily, Dr Cassidy paid her a special tribute

> Mother Teresa of Calcutta, you remind us of many things and challenge us to great things. In all sorts of ways you are the conscience of the world. We thank you for visiting us in Ireland and at Knock. We salute the work you do, the work of your Missionaries of Charity and of like minded people all over the world.

St Thérèse once said: 'I would like to travel over the whole world to preach your name ... to preach the Gospel on all five continents.'

Thérèse's wish has been fulfilled. In 1995 the Relics of St Thérèse of Lisieux began a pilgrimage of grace that will eventually cover the four corners of the world.

The Relics arrived in Knock Shrine on 8 June 2001. Not since the visit of Pope John Paul II in 1979 were there anything like the crowds present. It was the first great pilgrimage of the new millennium, accurately called 'A Pilgrimage of Grace'.

> *Fáilte Romat, a Threasa Óg*
> *Fáilte Romat, a Threasa Óg*
> *Céad Fáilte chuig Tranquilla*

– sang the Carmelite Sisters of Knock as the reliquary of St Thérèse of Lisieux arrived at their convent on 8 June 2001. Local people and the Carmelite community united in welcome and prayer.

> Our small chapel provided an intimate setting and allowed space for quiet prayer. So many people thanked us for allowing them to enter our space for a while, but it was our joy and privilege.

On 9 June the Relics of St Thérèse arrived in procession from the Carmelite Monastery to a packed Basilica. They were welcomed by Archbishop Michael Neary and Monsignor Grealy. On Sunday, 10 June, numbers were further increased when pilgrims from Down and Connor, led by Bishop Anthony Farquhar arrived for their annual pilgrimage. Day and night thousands of pilgrims thronged Knock to venerate the relics; each brought a rose as a symbol of their love and devotion. All present spoke of an atmosphere of reverence and devotion throughout the visit.

People queued for hours to file past the casket, to touch it, kiss it, press their roses to it and take them home as treasured keepsakes. The invalids, the young, the old – and in many cases the sceptics – were patient participants in an unparalleled event. Throughout the visit, huge numbers of people went to confession – reconciliation and healing in an atmosphere of shared peace and contentment.

It was not just the huge numbers present that recalled the days of the Papal visit in 1979. One of the gifts of Pope John Paul II to the Shrine was the precious Golden Rose. Every image of St Thérèse of Lisieux shows her with an armful of roses – The Little Flower – who declared

after my death I shall make a shower of roses rain down

and that is exactly what the pilgrims of Knock Shrine witnessed on those amazing days in June 2001.

What are highlights? Is it the sick child smiling briefly during the day, or the ailing parent/husband/wife/friend who finds some peace and returns home calmer than when they arrived? Perhaps it is the carer who finds the strength

to keep going for just another while. Perhaps, for those who work and pray daily for the ongoing development of devotion to Knock Shrine, it is seeing the thousands of pilgrims from all nations, participating in each new season.

Every visitor is special, whether they arrive as a searching individual, or as part of an organised national or international pilgrimage. Each person takes home his or her own personal memory. It may be the story they shared with another pilgrim, a few stolen hours of much needed peace and reflection, and perhaps a decision made. For each individual their pilgrimage has its own special highlight.

> Knock Shrine is a holy place because it has been favoured in a special way by God and His Mother. But it is also a holy place because it is the centre of such a massive volume of fervent prayer
> Monsignor Michael Walsh – *The Glory of Knock*

Look to this day,
For it is life,
The very life of life.
In its brief course lie all
The realities and verities of existence,
The bliss of growth, the splendour
Of action, the glory of power.

For yesterday is but a dream,
And tomorrow is only a vision.
But today, well lived,
Makes every yesterday a dream of happiness
And every tomorrow a vision of hope.
Look well, therefore, to this day.

Sanskrit proverb

KNOCK SHRINE is recognised today as a world-class Marian Shrine. The continuing development of the facilities required for today's pilgrims is an on-going process. Those who promote the shrine today are aware of the dedicated and practical groundwork laid down by decades of committed people.

In 1929, fifty years after the Apparition, little had changed around Knock. There were special devotions to celebrate the Golden Jubilee, and present at them were a young married couple from the locality, District Justice Liam Coyne and his wife, Judy. Subsequently, while visiting Lourdes in 1934 they became aware of the potential of Knock as a centre of devotion and prayer. At the blessing of the sick in Lourdes, they were inspired by the reverence and deeply prayerful responses of the invalids. They were extremely impressed at what was available for pilgrims and invalids in Lourdes and asked themselves 'Why should all this not be possible in Knock?' And so was planted the seed that blossomed into a life-long commitment to develop and promote Our Lady's Shrine at Knock to all nations.

On their return home they met Canon Grealy in Knock who suggested a meeting with Dr Gilmartin, Archbishop of Tuam. He encouraged them to start their campaign with a leaflet giving details of the Apparition and selected prayers. Within a very short time over half a million leaflets were distributed around Ireland, England, Scotland and some to America. They drove hundreds of miles around Ireland and were constantly amazed and gratified at the response of the public. Liam Coyne then agreed to write a book about Knock. This involved meetings with surviving witnesses, research in the National Library and interviews with people who claimed cures. Finally, in

November 1935, the book *Knock Shrine* was published. Other publications followed, including an account of the life of Archdeacon Cavanagh, Parish Priest of Knock during the time of the Apparition. In 1938 the *Knock Shrine Annual,* which continues today, was launched. Mrs Coyne edited the first edition and continued as editor until 1996 when Tom Neary, Chief Steward, took over. When Liam Coyne gave the first broadcast talk on Radio Éireann about Knock, he was approached by a leading Dublin consultant, Dr Stafford Johnson who suggested setting up a Medical Bureau at Knock. With the approval of the Archbishop and a team of doctors, all on a voluntary basis, the Bureau was established in 1937.

Other events to promote the Shrine included a broadcast symposium from the Gaiety Theatre in Dublin in December 1936. They even commissioned a 16 mm film made by Dr Jack Lyons of Kilkelly for use when giving lecture tours about Knock. By now, pilgrim numbers and the work relating to them had grown to such an extent that more helpers were needed. With the encouragement of Canon Grealy and the permission of Dr Gilmartin, the Society for Promoting the Cause of Knock Shrine – Knock Shrine Society – was founded and had their first meeting on 21 August 1935.

At this time, the Committee of Handmaids and Stewards was established. Looking at the Shrine's excellent facilities for pilgrims and invalids today, it is almost impossible to imagine the conditions of the mid-1930s. Like many other villages of the time, Knock had no electricity, no main water supply and no toilets. Starting with basic wooden huts, the volunteers boiled kettles on paraffin stoves, prepared food in their own homes and tried to cope with the constantly increasing numbers. Mrs Coyne dealt with all the queries relating to the Shrine. This she continued alone after her husband died in 1953. When Monsignor James Horan was appointed Parish Priest in Knock in 1967, he organised the present structure of offices and staff to cope with the running of the Shrine.

The involvement of the Handmaids and Stewards in the Shrine has continued to play a vital role down through the years – as noted by Pope John Paul II, on his visit during the centenary celebrations of 1979

> I know from first hand experience the value of the service you render to make every pilgrim feel at home at this Shrine, and to help them to make every visit a loving and prayerful encounter with Mary, the Mother of Divine Grace.

In light of the development of the Shrine into a new millennium, it is fascinating to note that at the Society's meeting of 20 October 1935, it was decided, as a priority, to enhance the Apparition Gable, to improve facilities at the shrine, as well as rail services, roads, a railway station – and to reserve a site for an airfield. Writing about those early days, in the 1995 Knock Shrine Annual – Mrs Coyne notes

> That airfield proposal, which was reported widely in the local papers, caused as much derision in its day, as did the Knock airport in more recent years.

The first St Joseph's Rest House was opened in 1957 and replaced by a much larger building in 1971. It provided a spiritual week for invalids, and was staffed by 'dedicated' special volunteers, who had devoted their lives to this special work of charity. This work now continues under the care of the St John of God Brothers. St Mary's Hostel, run by the Daughters of Charity, provides accommodation for pilgrims throughout the pilgrimage season.

The Apparition statues, now enshrined at the gable wall of the old church, were commissioned in 1960, with the permission of Dr Joseph Walsh, Archbishop of Tuam, by the Handmaids and Stewards, to mark their Silver Jubilee. Following an open competition, Professor Lorenzo Ferri from Rome was commissioned to carve the statues. From the very beginning he was committed to the project. The statues are carved in white Carrara marble, giving them an almost luminous quality. Monsignor D. Conway, then in the Irish College in Rome and subsequently Bishop of Elphin, liaised with the sculptor, translating the accounts of the Apparition into Italian for him. Mrs Coyne had many conversations with one visionary, Mrs Mary O'Connell, who described in detail for her, the size, position, clothing and expressions of the figures. In her own account of the carving of the statues Mrs Coyne recalls

> She [Mary O'Connell] had a wonderful memory and remarked at one time that she could close her eyes and see the vision all over again.
> Siobhán Bean Uí Cadhain – *The Vision in Marble*

When the time came to give the final verdict on the statues, November 1960, Dr Walsh asked Mrs Coyne to go to Rome to see the figures. While generally pleased with them, she was unhappy with the expression on Our Lady's face,

and felt that the Lamb did not resemble an Irish lamb – he was definitely Italian. Mrs Coyne found an 'Irish looking' lamb in the Italian hills and brought him to the studio where he was used as a model for the Apparition lamb. Around this time, Professor Ferri became ill. Mrs Coyne stayed on in Rome and was invited to travel to San Giovanni Rotundo to attend Padre Pio's Mass, where she prayed for Professor Ferri's recovery.

On her return she was delighted to see the sculptor recovered and pronounced the statue of Our Lady perfect. The statues were delivered to Knock, in a downpour, on the eve of 8 September 1963.

The 'Irish looking' lamb became a much loved pet of the Sisters of the Little Company of Mary and lived out his life in the hills around their convent at Fiesole near Florence.

Back in Knock, the Handmaids and Stewards continued their work of promoting the Shrine. Today, they maintain this work with the same dedication as in former days. At the beginning of each season they have a day of recollection to ask for God's blessing and then end the season with a day of thanksgiving. Each Sunday begins with Mass in the Blessed Sacrament Chapel and the recitation of their special Morning Offering. Their care for and devotion to the invalids is of immense importance, especially in the Basilica on the great pilgrimage days when they assist the invalids seated around the altar, or in wheelchairs or lying on stretchers.

Mrs Coyne was a person who throughout her life shunned publicity; sixty years after founding the Knock Shrine Society she wrote

The Golden Rose presented by Pope John Paul II during his centenary visit

In all of our work for Knock, my husband Liam and I always had a very firm conviction that Providence guided our every step, and I remain convinced that were it not for the direction of the Holy Spirit, we could never have undertaken and continued with it.

Knock Shrine Annual 1995

However, her work and involvement with the Shrine has been acknowledged by the Church. In 1984 she was presented with the medal *Pro Ecclesia et Pontifice* ('For Church and Pope') – the highest honour a Pope can bestow on a woman. Then, on 7 September 1997, Archbishop Michael Neary presented her with the Certificate and Medal, conferred on her by Pope John Paul II, granting her the title 'Grand-Dame of the Order of St Sylvester'.

Today's pilgrims make a visit to the new Apparition Chapel at the gable wall of the old church the focal point of their trip to Knock. The old church itself is also well worth visiting. It has a prayerful atmosphere of timelessness. It was in that very building that the visionaries would have gathered for Mass and where, after the Apparition, thousands of people continuously gathered to give thanks and pray. Archdeacon Cavanagh's grave is there, with a memorial tablet in Latin outlining the qualities of a much loved parish priest. The Harry Clarke stained glass window depicts Our Lady of Mount Carmel presenting the Brown Scapular to St Simon Stock. The window was blessed and unveiled on 27 August 1961 in Memory of Fr Rabbitte OCarm, Whitefriar Street, Dublin. Cured at Knock as a young boy, he organised the first Carmelite pilgrimage to Knock and continued to do so throughout his life. Outside on the gable wall the Golden Rose, presented by Pope John Paul II during his centenary visit, is permanently displayed.

The pilgrimage season in Knock starts on the last Sunday in April and runs until the second Sunday in October inclusive. Today, the visitor to Knock Shrine can structure their visit to suit their personal needs. Those there for just one day, particularly a busy pilgrimage day, need to plan their time carefully. The booklet titled *The Pilgrims Guide* is just what it says – a complete guide to all the services available, all the Devotions, Mass times, Confessions, Novenas, Vigils, a location map of the various buildings, and an outline of the Traditional Station performed by the pilgrim. The Station starts with a visit to the Blessed Sacrament in any of the chapels, followed by the Stations of the Cross. Reflections on each station are available in the guide. Traditionally, the pilgrim then recites the Fifteen Mysteries of the Rosary – Joyful, Sorrowful and Glorious – while walking around the church anti-clockwise. Sometimes pilgrims say the Joyful Mysteries on the journey to the Shrine, and the Glorious Mysteries on the way home. The Litany of the Blessed Virgin, the Prayer to Our Lady of Knock, followed by a visit to the Blessed Sacrament where the Creed and the prayer to Christ the King is recited concludes this traditional devotion at the Shrine.

The National Novena in honour of Our Lady of Knock takes place from 14 to 22 August inclusive each year. Two of the biggest feastdays on the Knock calendar are celebrated during the Novena – The Feast of the Assumption on 15 August and the Feast of Our Lady of Knock on 21 August. During the Novena week there is a planned programme of talks from invited speakers on a range of topics relevant to today's pilgrims. Twice daily there are the traditional liturgies of Knock in the Basilica. This National Novena is one of the highlights of the Pilgrimage Season and attracts thousands of visitors each day.

Confessions are available every day in the Chapel of Reconciliation where pilgrims can also avail of the counselling services, either by making an appointment or by calling in to the centre in the Chapel of Reconciliation.

During the Pilgrimage Season pilgrims can reflect and pray in the Guided Prayer Centre. There are three sessions each day. A passage of Scripture is read by a trained prayer guide and, in an atmosphere of quiet reflection, participants can meditate on the word of God as it touches each one personally. All ages drop in to the centre not knowing what to expect or experience, and find that they return again to pray and listen in the calming presence of a loving God. Should they so wish, they can meet with a prayer guide to discuss their prayer life, perhaps resolve any difficulties they might have and possibly discover how they could continue to use the process of guided prayer when they return home. Within the centre is the Audio Visual Centre, where a variety of relevant films are screened.

Behind the Stations of the Cross, near Our Lady's Garden, is the Blessed Sacrament Chapel. Built exclusively for the Blessed Sacrament and its adoration, it is a quiet haven for prayer, and is particularly relevant to the Knock Apparition and devotion.

And rest aside in Him
Enter the inner chamber of your soul
Shut out everything except God
And that which can help you in seeking Him
Now, my whole heart, say to God,
I seek your face,
Lord it is your face I seek.
  Dreaming with Tony de Mello

The Basilica is in use mainly during the Pilgrimage Season. It is an ideal venue for the thousands of pilgrims who partake in the many pilgrimages throughout the season. The invalids always have a special place in the Basilica where they have the assistance of the Handmaids and Stewards at all times. To participate at any of the big occasions there with the clergy, Handmaids, Stewards, choirs and the thousands of pilgrims, is to experience a tangible presence of the Sacred.

The Knock Ambulance Service began on 18 May 1975. Originally under the auspices of the Red Cross, it is now run by the Order of Malta and each season provides an invaluable service to the pilgrims at the Shrine.

Facilitating the pilgrims of tomorrow is organised through the services of an active Youth Ministry in Knock. There are regular Pilgrimages for schools and youth organisations, each one specifically designed for a different age group. Young people who go to Knock have an opportunity to step aside from the day-to-day routine of life, to reflect on God, on themselves and take stock of their lives in a positive, and encouraging environment.

The story of the Apparition at Knock in the context of those bygone times is fully explored in the Folk Museum. Situated in the Shrine grounds with a full time professional curator available to assist the visitor, it is a fascinating opportunity to see the lives, trades and artifacts, both lay and religious, of long-gone years. The old cemetery near the Museum contains graves of several of the Apparition witnesses, adding a further link to the past.

During the pilgrimage season, the Shrine grounds are a constant source of joy and inspiration. The grounds are planned by the head gardener and grounds staff to provide an all year round back-drop for the Shrine. For any pilgrim who wants to take time to go apart from the crowds and find a quiet space, the combination of layout, colour and scent with a background of birdsong, provides a ready-made haven of peace and tranquility.

Within the grounds there is now a sheltered housing scheme for the elderly.

From March to October, tourists in the area can avail of the first-class caravan and camping park, equipped to the highest standards with all the modern facilities required for today's visitor. The park is a member of the Irish Caravan and Camping Council. Sponsored by Bord Failte, the park is also a caravan club size, and was awarded the Ambience Award in 2001.

The addition of the excellently equipped, three-star Knock House Hotel with a full range of facilities is a welcome addition for the discerning visitor to the area. Situated beside the shrine, it has a full range of invalid facilities and a medical centre within the hotel. Open all year round, it provides comfort and care in an ideal location.

Within the Shrine complex there is a complete range of facilities designed to answer the needs of the enormous variety of pilgrims visiting the Shrine.

The Knock Shrine Offices within the grounds will provide information on any of the Associations relating to the Shrine

> Knock Shrine Friends' Association
> Knock Shrine International Blessed Sacrament Guild
> The Eucharistic Legion
> Knock Shrine Rosary Crusade.

Pilgrims Guides are available in Irish, French, German, Italian, Spanish, Portuguese and Polish.

The Knock Marriage Introductions Bureau was established in 1968. It is authorised by the Archbishop and Bishops of Connaught and under the patronage of Our Lady of Knock. All applicants are treated in the strictest confidence by the Secretary of the Bureau. Since its establishment, the Bureau has averaged twenty-two marriages each year with applicants from every county in Ireland and all professions.

The Family Life and Prayer Centre is beside the North Ambulatory of the Basilica beside the North Main Entrance and provides information on Family Prayer, Family Planning (STMI) Pro-Life, Counselling, Marriage Encounter and a Library.

On Sundays, priests and sisters are available at the Religious Vocations Centre to advise on vocations to the priesthood and religious life. This centre is at the right hand side of the Basilica.

The Bookcentre is located opposite the Blessed Sacrament Chapel and carries an extensive range of religious publications, including Knock Shrine publications. There is also a range of videos, including the official video of the Shrine – *The Story of Knock* – together with CDs and tapes.

Pilgrims from around the world can, thanks to today's technical advances, stay in touch with Knock through their computer.
Email: info@knock-shrine.ie
or visit the web-side at http://www.knock-shrine.ie

HAIL MARY   Hail Mary, full of grace,
               The Lord is with thee.
               Blessed art thou among women
               And blessed is the fruit of thy womb, Jesus.
               Holy Mary, mother of God,
               Pray for us sinners,
               Now, and at the hour of our death.
               Amen.

CONDUCT OF PILGRIMAGES

Pilgrimages must always have a truly religious character.
Pilgrimages should be made in a spirit of fervent prayer, self-denial and recollection.

PLENARY INDULGENCE FOR PILGRIMS

Pilgrims may gain a Plenary Indulgence:
1. On the Feast of Our Lady of Knock. (21 August)
2. On one other day in the year. (The choice of day is left to each individual.)
3. Conditions: Pilgrims must be in the state of grace, have received Holy Communion and must pray for the intentions of Our Holy Father, the Pope. (One Our Father, Hail Mary and Glory Be to the Father)
4. The Our Father and Creed must be recited at the Shrine.

PROGRAMME OF DEVOTIONS PILGRIMAGE SEASON

Last Sunday April – Second Sunday October inclusive

Sundays and Holydays
Masses: 8, 9.30 and 11 am 12 noon, 3 and 7 pm
               Eve of Sundays and Holydays 7.30 pm
Confessions: Continuously from 11 am to 7 pm in The Chapel of Reconciliation. It is not necessary for pilgrims who have already gone to confession elsewhere to go to confession

again at Knock Shrine in order to gain the Indulgence
Public Ceremonies: 2.30 pm Anointing of the Sick. 3 pm
Concelebrated Mass followed by the Solemn Blessing of the
Sick, Benediction of the Blessed Sacrament, Rosary
Procession to the Shrine and blessing of pious objects.

Weekdays

Masses: 8, 9 and 11 am 12 noon, 3, 5, and 7.30 pm
Confessions: Monday to Friday continuously from 11 am to 5 pm
               (August: 11 am to 6 pm)
Saturdays   11 am to 9 pm in the Chapel of Reconciliation.

Public Ceremonies:

               2.15 pm Stations of the Cross and Rosary Procession
               3 pm Concelebrated Mass with Anointing of the Sick

EXPOSITION OF THE BLESSED SACRAMENT

Daily in the Blessed Sacrament Chapel after 11 am Mass until 5 pm (May to
October)

LAST THURSDAY OF EACH MONTH FOR INVALIDS

2.15 pm   Stations of the Cross and Rosary Procession
3 pm   Concelebrated Mass with special homily dealing with the
               vocation of suffering and Anointing of the Sick
4 pm   Blessing of the Sick and Benediction of the Blessed Sacrament.

ALL NIGHT PUBLIC VIGILS – (First Friday of Month)

May, June, July, August, September, October and 7 December.

ALL NIGHT PUBLIC VIGIL PROGRAMME

10pm-12 midnight	Confessions in Chapel of Reconciliation
12 midnight	Introductory Prayer and Welcome
12.10–12.45 am	Service of Prayer and Thanksgiving
12.45–1.30 am	Rosary and Candlelight Procession
1.30–2.30 am	Holy Hour
2.30–3 am	Private Prayer outside in silence
3–3.40 am	Conducted Stations of the Cross in the Basilica
3.40–4 am	Preparation for Mass
4 am	Concelebrated Mass

VIGIL RULES:	Silence must be observed at all times
	No food or drink other than water can be taken during the vigil hours. No smoking permitted.

THE NATIONAL NOVENA IN HONOUR OF OUR LADY OF KNOCK
14 to 22 August (inclusive)

AFTERNOON:

3 pm	Concelebrated Mass in the Basilica, Novena Prayers, Eucharistic Blessing of the Sick, Procession of the Blessed Sacrament to Apparition Chapel.

EVENING:

> 8.30 pm Concelebrated Mass in the Basilica, Novena Prayers, Candlelight Procession to Apparition Chapel.
> Those unable to attend the ceremonies at the Shrine may join in the Novena by reciting the Novena Prayers and the Rosary. Mass and Holy Communion in the local Church is also recommended.
> Novena prayer leaflets and booklets may be had from the Shrine Office.

FEAST OF THE ASSUMPTION – 15 AUGUST

Masses: 6, 7, 8, 9, 9.30, 10 and 11 am, 12 noon, 1, 3, 7 and 8.30 pm
>   Anointing of the sick: 2.30 pm
>   Confessions: Continuously from 5 am – 8 pm in Chapel of Reconciliation

WINTER PROGRAMME

From second Sunday October – Last Sunday April

Sundays & Holydays:

>   Masses: 9 and 11 am, 12, 3 and 5 pm
>   (Eve of Sundays and Holydays 7.30 pm)
>   Confessions: 11 am, 1 pm and 2 pm to 5 pm
>   Weekdays: Masses: 9, 11 am, 12, 3 and 5 pm
>   Confessions: 11 am to 1 pm and 2 to 5 pm